This BASICS book™
belongs to

....

....

....

Great Britain
Europe
The Universe
The Galaxy

Published exclusively for
Tesco Stores Limited
Cheshunt
EN8 9SL
by David Bennett Books Limited
94 Victoria Street
St Albans
Herts AL1 3TG

First published in 1990 by
David Bennett Books Limited

Art Director: Steve Avery
Series Editor: Ruth Thomson
Picture researcher: Rachel Wright
Consultants: Professor W. M. Blaney,
Department of Biology, Birkbeck College, University of London;
The Natural History Museum, London

Printed in Hong Kong

ISBN: 1 - 85602 - 002 - 9

**Don't worry! We have drawn most of the creepy crawlies
in this book much larger than they are in real life.
This is so you can see what they really look like.**

Creepy Crawlies

Written by

Ruth Thomson

Illustrated by

Dom Mansell

TESCO · Bennett

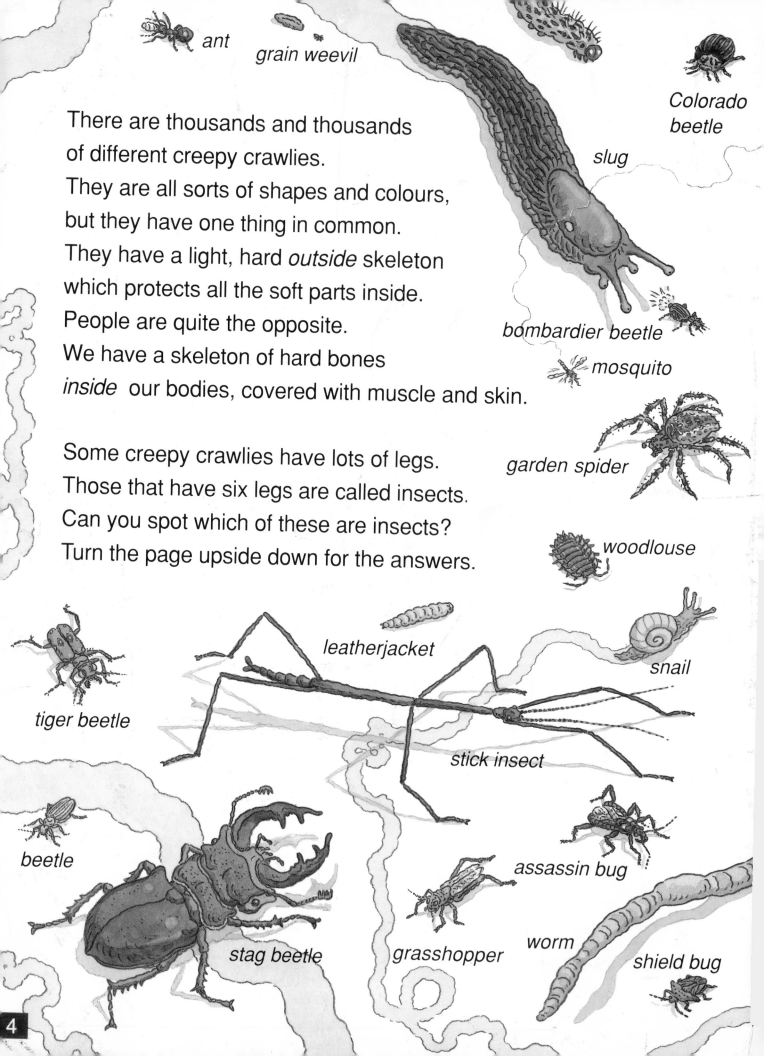

ant

grain weevil

Colorado beetle

slug

There are thousands and thousands
of different creepy crawlies.
They are all sorts of shapes and colours,
but they have one thing in common.
They have a light, hard *outside* skeleton
which protects all the soft parts inside.
People are quite the opposite.
We have a skeleton of hard bones
inside our bodies, covered with muscle and skin.

Some creepy crawlies have lots of legs.
Those that have six legs are called insects.
Can you spot which of these are insects?
Turn the page upside down for the answers.

bombardier beetle

mosquito

garden spider

woodlouse

leatherjacket

snail

tiger beetle

stick insect

beetle

assassin bug

stag beetle

grasshopper

worm

shield bug

long-horned
beetle

lacewing

ladybird

cricket

centipede

scorpion

house spider

locust

snail

dor beetle

pill millipede

millipede

mole cricket

earwig

puss moth caterpillar

emperor moth

ladybird larva

greenfly

fly

cockchafer
beetle

bed bug

beetle

The insects are: caterpillar (they have six real legs and 10 false ones), earwig, weevil,
cricket, grasshopper, ant, ladybird, greenfly, beetles, bugs, mosquito, leatherjacket,
lacewing, locust, mole cricket, moth.

5

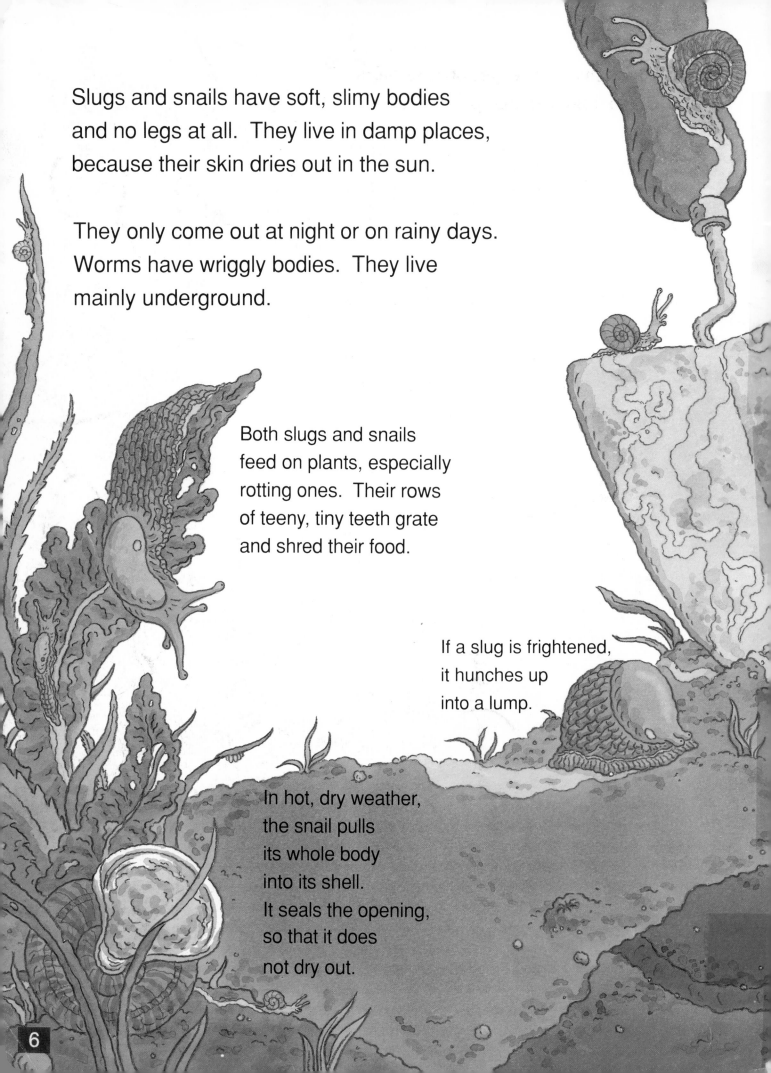

Slugs and snails have soft, slimy bodies
and no legs at all. They live in damp places,
because their skin dries out in the sun.

They only come out at night or on rainy days.
Worms have wriggly bodies. They live
mainly underground.

Both slugs and snails
feed on plants, especially
rotting ones. Their rows
of teeny, tiny teeth grate
and shred their food.

If a slug is frightened,
it hunches up
into a lump.

In hot, dry weather,
the snail pulls
its whole body
into its shell.
It seals the opening,
so that it does
not dry out.

Slugs and snails have eyes on long stalks.
If they are disturbed, they pull their eyes in.

Slugs and snails move slowly.
Their wide, muscular foot
ripples and pushes them forwards.
They make a layer of sticky
slime under their foot.
This helps them to move
easily over rough surfaces.

If the tail of a worm is cut off,
it can grow back again.

Worms pull dead leaves
into their burrows to eat.

Worms eat soil,
as they tunnel underground.
Sometimes you will see little heaps
of fine soil on the ground.
These have been left by worms.
They are called worm-casts.

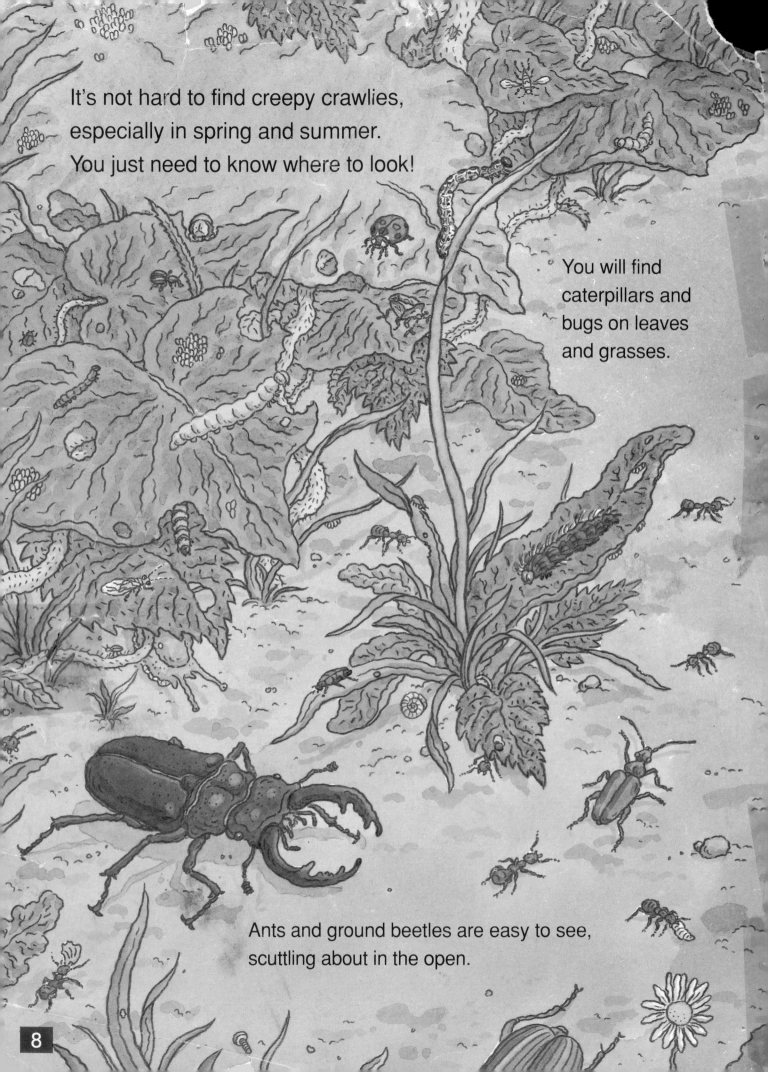

It's not hard to find creepy crawlies,
especially in spring and summer.
You just need to know where to look!

You will find
caterpillars and
bugs on leaves
and grasses.

Ants and ground beetles are easy to see,
scuttling about in the open.

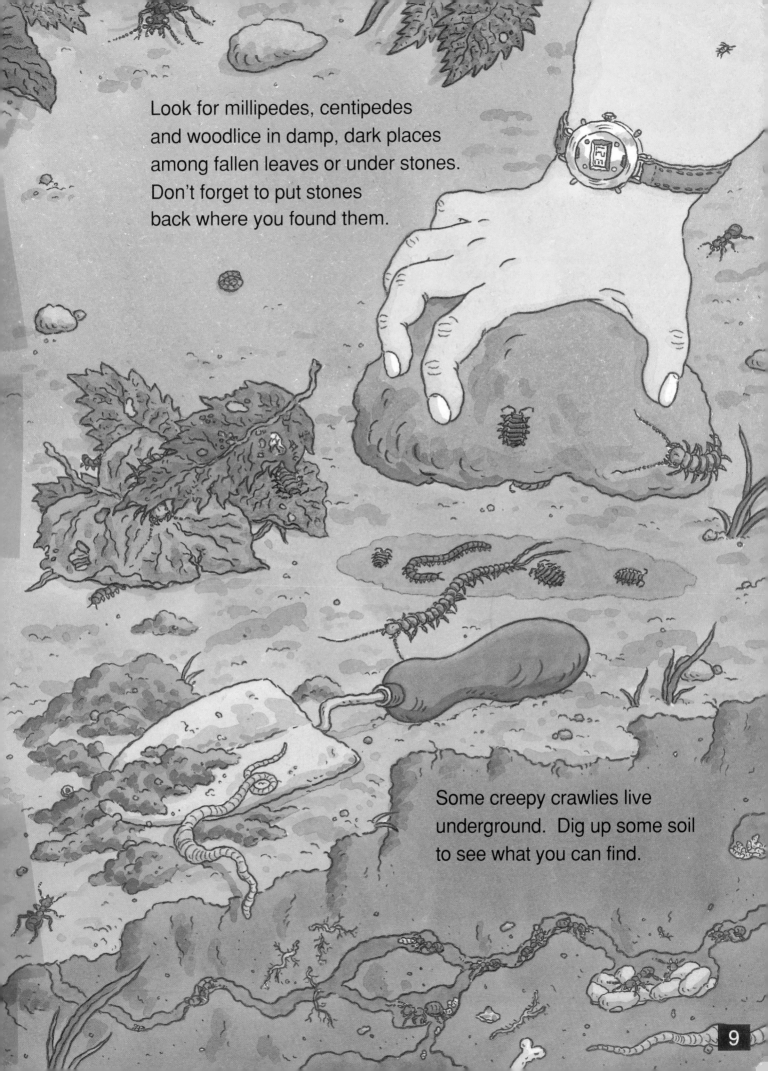

Look for millipedes, centipedes
and woodlice in damp, dark places
among fallen leaves or under stones.
Don't forget to put stones
back where you found them.

Some creepy crawlies live
underground. Dig up some soil
to see what you can find.

Creepy crawlies spend a lot of their time eating.

Caterpillars and beetles have strong, ridged jaws for biting and chewing.

Bugs, flies and mosquitoes have a hollow tube, rather like a drinking straw, for sucking liquids.

buff tip moth caterpillar

birch

Caterpillars munch leaves. Each kind of caterpillar has a favourite sort of plant on which it likes to feed.

cabbage white

peacock

small tortoiseshell

cabbage

nettle

These flower beetles eat the pollen inside flowers.

Woodlice and millipedes feed mainly on rotting plants.

woodlouse

millipede

Greenfly make holes in plant stems and leaves and suck out the sap from inside.

These creepy crawlies
eat other creepy crawlies.

The assassin bug jabs its sharp mouth
into its prey and sucks the juices inside.

The scorpion seizes insects and spiders
in its big claws and stings them to death
before eating them.

This tiger beetle is very fierce.
It runs fast to catch ants, bugs and flies
in its strong jaws. It kills its victims
by banging them
on the ground.

This spider has spun a sticky web of silk.
It waits quietly until a juicy fly lands on the web.

When the fly struggles to escape,
the spider poisons it with a bite, so it can't move,
and then wraps it in silk. The spider stores the fly
alive in the web until it feels hungry.

Almost all creepy crawlies hatch from eggs. The eggs of ants, beetles and butterflies hatch into wriggly larvae, which don't look at all like adult insects. Let's see what happens.

These ladybirds are mating.

The female lays her eggs on a leaf.

The eggs hatch into tiny larvae.

The larvae eat greenfly. They eat and eat and eat. As they eat, they grow.

As a larva grows, its skin becomes too tight. A new soft skin grows underneath.

The old skin splits and the larva wriggles and pulls its way out in its new skin. This is called moulting.

The new skin is soft at first.
The larva can stretch into it.
Later the skin hardens.

The larva moults four times.
Orange markings appear
on its body.

It grows very fat. It stops eating.
It stops growing.

It finds a safe place under a leaf
and fixes itself to the stem.

Its skin splits one last time
and the larva turns into a pupa.

Inside the pupa, an amazing
change takes place. The pupa
turns into a ladybird.

The ladybird pushes itself
out of the pupa.
Its body is soft and pale.

Slowly its body dries.
Its wing cases harden
and its spots appear.

Some creepy crawlies hatch
looking like small adults,
but they don't have wings.
They are called nymphs.

cricket

cricket nymph

shield bug

shield bug nymph

earwig nymph

earwig

A grasshopper nymph moults several times
before it is fully grown. Each time it moults,
it gets bigger...

 and bigger ...

 and bigger ...

and bigger.

And each time it moults,
its wing buds grow a little more.
At the last moult, the wings are fully grown
and it is an adult. It doesn't grow any more.

Creepy crawlies don't have noses, ears, fingers
or tongues. Their eyes are quite different from ours.
But they can still smell, hear, touch, taste and see!

Insects taste and smell with their antennae.
These are the prongs on the front of their heads.
Antennae are all shapes and sizes.

They can be feathery...

emperor moth

long and thin...

long-horned beetle

or fan-shaped.

cockchafer beetle

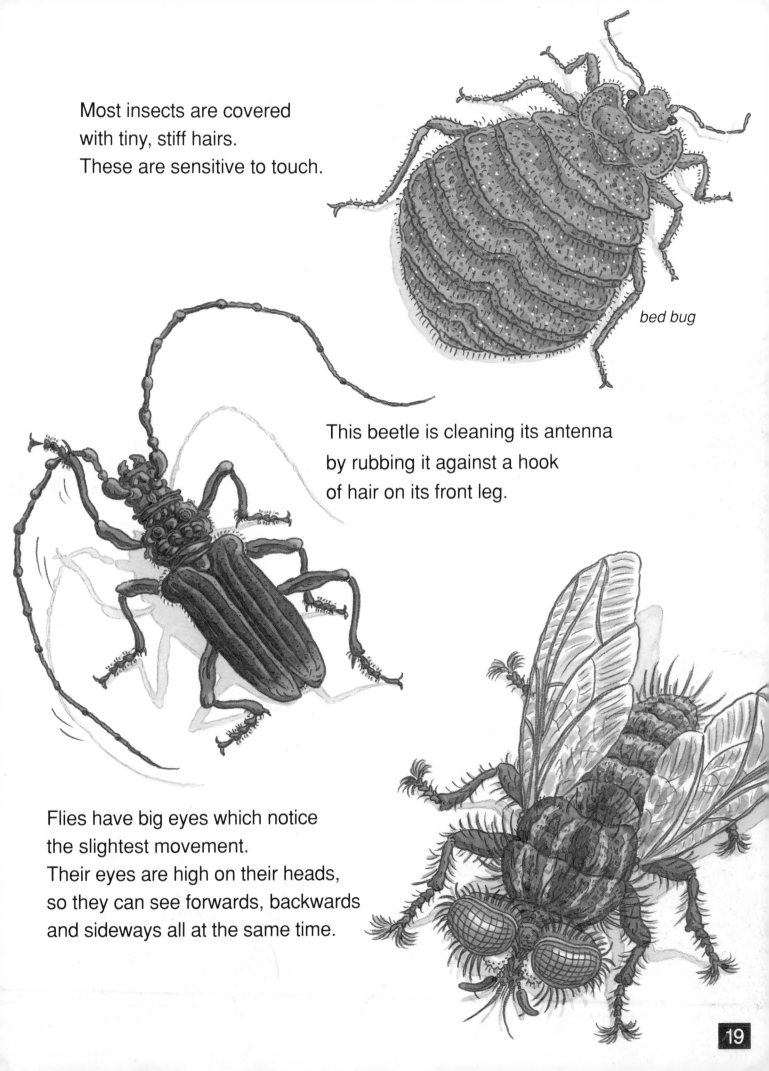

Most insects are covered
with tiny, stiff hairs.
These are sensitive to touch.

bed bug

This beetle is cleaning its antenna
by rubbing it against a hook
of hair on its front leg.

Flies have big eyes which notice
the slightest movement.
Their eyes are high on their heads,
so they can see forwards, backwards
and sideways all at the same time.

One thing you're sure to notice
is that many creepy crawlies are
always on the move.

ladybird

You may be surprised that some beetles can fly.
Under their hard wing cases are wings.
The beetles fold their wings back
under their wing cases when they land.

wing case

stag beetle

wing

Some hunters run fast
in their search for prey.

tiger beetle

Most creepy crawlies have legs
that are all the same size.

Ones that jump
have long back legs.

grasshopper

Those that dig
have short, strong
front legs.

mole cricket

centipede

Did you know that if a spider
or a young stick insect loses a leg,
it can grow a new one?

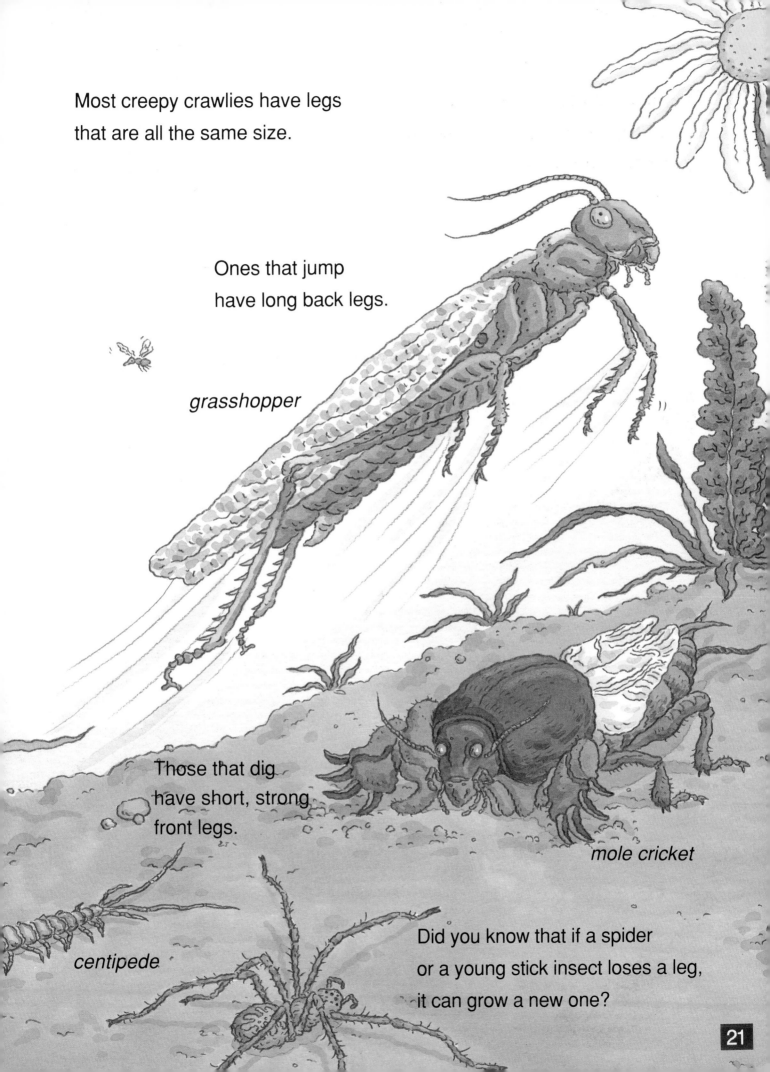

Creepy crawlies have ways of protecting
themselves against hungry enemies.

Some creepy crawlies are the same colour
and shape as their surroundings.
This is called camouflage. Try saying it.
When they keep still, they are hard to spot.
Can you see a stick insect, a caterpillar,
a moth and a grasshopper hiding
in this picture?

A pill millipede curls
itself into a tight ball
if it is disturbed.

Enemies mainly attack creepy crawlies which move. So in times of danger, they pull in their legs and lie very still. Can you see a spider and a ladybird protecting themselves like this?

Some creepy crawlies can give an enemy a big surprise.

The puss moth caterpillar raises its head and looks frightening.

The bombardier beetle fires out a loud pop and a smelly puff of smoke.

Most creepy crawlies live alone,
but ants live together, thousands and
thousands of them, in underground nests.
A queen starts the nest. She lays all the eggs.
Worker ants look after her and the nest.
Each ant has its own job, which changes
as it grows older.

Ants are good at
finding their way
about. They leave a
scent trail to food for
other ants to follow.

Some workers fetch
twigs and bits of leaf
to mend the nest.
The part underground
is covered with a mound
of twigs which keeps it
warm and dry.

Ants beware!
This lurking beetle
is after you.

Ants love sweet foods.
Greenfly make a sugary
juice called honeydew,
which the ants like to eat.

They put rubbish
in special chambers
or take it outside the nest.

Adult ants have wings.
They fly off to mate.

Ants can tell by
their smell which ants
belong to their nest.
They fight and squirt
acid at strangers.

Ants rub antennae
when they meet
to find out if they are
from the same nest.

Older workers
bring back food
for feeding to
the larvae.

Ants eat almost
anything -
caterpillars,
beetles, flies
and woodlice.

When the queen ant lays her eggs,
the worker ants take them away to warmer
chambers, where they will hatch into larvae.

Younger workers
feed the larvae
and lick them clean.

The larvae turn into cocoons.
The worker ants bite them
open when the ants are ready
to come out.

Some creepy crawlies can be very helpful
to us, while others are pests.
The helpful ones feed on some of the pests,
help improve the soil and tidy up.
The pests eat farmers' crops, destroy wood
and pass on diseases.

Can you guess which of these creepy crawlies
are goodies and which are baddies?

Lacewings and ladybirds
eat the greenfly
which can spoil plants.
Every ladybird eats 30
greenfly a day.

Grain weevils spoil stored grain.
They bore into the seeds
with their snouts and lay eggs
inside. The larvae feed on the grain.

The Colorado beetle, which lives
in America, attacks potato crops.

A swarm of locusts can destroy
a whole year's crop in a few hours.

Dung beetles bury animal dung
and lay their eggs in it.
Their larvae feed on the dung
when they hatch.

Leatherjackets (the larvae of cranefly)
live underground in damp soil.
They feed on the roots and stems
of peas, beans and cereal crops.

Ladybirds, lacewings and dung beetles are goodies.
Colorado beetles, grain weevils, leatherjackets
and locusts are baddies.

Collect some creepy crawlies
for a little while to have a closer look.
They are very fragile, so don't hold them for long.
Use a soft brush to push them gently into a jar or box.
The best container for creepy crawlies is a fish tank.
Cover it with muslin, or a lid with plenty of holes.

A home for caterpillars

Put a jar in a cool place out
of the sun. Caterpillars need
fresh leaves every day.
Only give them the type of leaves
you found them on. If you can't,
it's best not to keep caterpillars,
because they will die.

A home for millipedes

Line the base of the tank
with damp compost, dead leaves,
rotting wood, twigs and bark.
Put in a shallow bowl of water with
cotton wool in it. Feed the millipedes
with little bits of raw fruit and
vegetable peelings.

A home for ladybirds

Ladybirds eat greenfly, which you will find on many garden plants, especially roses. Cut whole shoots and stand them in water to keep them fresh.

A home for a black ground beetle

Only keep *one* beetle at a time.
Line the tank with a deep layer
of damp soil (which you must keep damp).
Put in some large stones and a piece
of rotting wood for the beetle to hide under.
This beetle eats slugs and worms
or you could give it small pieces
of meat.

A home for grasshoppers

Be warned - grasshoppers are very tricky to catch. Keep them in a covered tank lined with sand or soil. Feed them daily with fresh grass.

Once you have finished looking
at creepy crawlies, put them back
exactly where you found them
or else they may die.

There goes the black ground beetle.

INDEX

BASICS

An introduction to our world